MESS & MUSE

UNNATII DUGGAL

Made with ♥ on the Notion Press Platform
www.notionpress.com

I dedicate this book to all the artists striving to create their finest work. Whether ascending from mess or inspired by a muse, never cease to create what you love.

Always remember, as an artist, you too are a work of art.

Contents

Contents

Contents

Acknowledgements

I thank the brilliant artists involved in the illustrations and editing process who carved my words into art.

I am grateful to my family, by blood and chosen; you have given me the courage to be true to myself.

I am grateful for the people who read my work and inspire me. You are the reason I continue to create.

From The Author's Desk

As a writer, my greatest strength has always been my unwavering commitment to writing, even when my doubts conspire against me. As an artist, I firmly believe that you can either admire your art without the weighing fear of judgement so it becomes the very reason you continue to create. Or, you could let the voices in and outside your head drag you down so profoundly that they become the reason you question everything you create or do.

Yet, as a human, I believe perseverance and catharsis are your best friends in pursuing your desires.

In much the same way, this book has been deeply cathartic for me in ways unexplained. Writing it, my mind wandered through two realms. In one, I explored the depths of loss and grief, and the mess it creates inside your head. In the other, I delved into the things and people I love so deeply, defining not only the idea of having them but admiring the muse they are.

When I take a step back and look at my life through a rose-coloured lens, I see all the worlds in my head coming together in my heart, and Mess And Muse is the heart I'm giving to the world.

The Playlist

- Love On The Brain ~ Rihanna
- Only Love Can Hurt Like This ~ Paloma Faith
- Just Give Me a Reason ~ Pink & Nate Ruess
- Daylight ~ David Kushner
- Bad Things ~ MGK & Camila Cabello
- Guilty As Sin ~ Taylor Swift
- About You - The 1975
- This is how you fall in love ~ Jeremy Zucker & Chelsea Cutter
- She Will Be Loved ~ Maroon 5
- No Promises ~ Shayne Ward
- Car's Outside ~ James Arthur
- Rivers and Roads ~ The Head and the Heart
- Elastic Heart ~ Sia
- Young and Beautiful ~ Lana Del Rey
- What Was I Made For? ~ Billie Eilish
- You Asked For This ~ Halsey
- You're On Your Own, Kid ~ Taylor Swift

Listen to the playlist in order as each song inspired the book-writing process and tells a story when heard together.

About The Artists

Nandika Mahajan as a designer, blends creativity and precision to craft pieces that go beyond aesthetics, telling stories and creating lasting impressions. Her work reflects a deep understanding of materials and a passion for transforming ideas into tangible, meaningful experiences. Design, for her, is about more than just beauty—it's about making connections and leaving a mark through the art of creation.

Abhijayaa Verma, a design student, is passionate about merging creativity with self-expression. Beyond academics, art is a central focus, with a love for experimenting with various styles and mediums. She enjoys baking, crafting DIY projects, creating handmade decorations, and custom jewelry, turning imaginative ideas into tangible creations. Reading is another cherished pastime that broadens her perspective, and she has a fascination with tattoos as powerful symbols of personal stories and artistic expression.

Sanjivani Sinha is a psychology major who finds joy in reading, writing, and mostly all art forms including sketching and painting. A lover of literature and poetry, she has a keen eye for creative content creation, styling, and singing. Her artistic talents and passion for visual storytelling have greatly contributed to curating the graphics for this poetry collection.

THE MESS

Growing up for me was not easy

Growing up is never easy for someone
Who understands the depths of every human emotion;
Especially when you're raised as a gifted child,
That's when all your potential turns to anger.

Growing up,
I was enclosed by expectations of excellence,
Accompanied by cheerful hoorays when I prevailed
But that was all a consequence of,
Isolation, insomnia, and, believe me, loneliness.

A part of me always assumed,
Whatever I achieved in grades,
Was all I could ever do.
Whatever I loved, mess or muse,
Was never good enough to be seen as art.

So I built walls around me,
Thinking they would protect me,
These walls did shield me for a long time,
Still, my mind echoed the truth:
If I never let myself truly bleed,
I am never going to heal,

So I welcomed the wounds and wears
Letting them scavenge my soul,
Until I became a mosaic of incompleteness,
My house turned into a home of emptiness,
My mind resents intellect until it's a mess.

You see, growing up was never easy to do,
But all along, it became all I could ever do.

I want answers

I swore at fifteen
I would work for a prominent corporation,
But at eighteen,
I am desperate to find out how the human mind works.

How can someone love you so selflessly
Yet tear you apart?
How can someone curse you for a long time
But still look after you?

How one day,
You can have the world in your hands
But the next day,
Your world could succumb to those hands.

I want answers on how someone can make you miserable
While simultaneously seeking healing from you;
I want answers to how one human
Can withstand so much pain,
And sublimate it into something haunting
Or something enchanting.

Loving at Nineteen

At nineteen,
I've never been as puzzled about love as I am now,
It's when the clock strikes at 2 a.m.

When I strain to fall asleep,
My mind and I try relentlessly to find.
The remedy for a broken heart,
Knowing what kills me is my remedy.

It's wild how we confessed to falling out of love,
But he still traces my hands with his fingers,
As our favourite songs play in his car.

I changed my hair and sacrificed what I loved,
I broke sacred promises and vows of fidelity,
There was someone on my mind,
Who could never be mine,
Yet, when his eyes met mine,
It felt like the ecstasy poets write about.

It's insane how a forbidden kiss
Could lead to soul-crushing farewells,
Along with hopelessness at the airport,
I lie awake questioning.
Every unthinkable scenario in my life
Praying for nothing but a heart to heal,
I let it break endlessly,
I peel back my skin;
The bare hands I touched him with,
Oscillating between a love
That was something and a love
That could have been something.

As I pour my heart out in words,
After months of silence,

Wars between my head and heart,
The melancholy runs through my racing heart,
Pacifying my soul.

It's ironic how words, my only power,
Could make me feel so weak and defenceless
As I write down the story of a girl,
Who made all the unfair choices in love.

I may break and fall; let me be

Walls of insecurities bind me,
A labyrinth of fears and doubts consumes me,
They cascade into sleepless midnights,
And empty mornings.

I tried to fill the voids of the touch of men on me,
With something stronger than drugs,
Manipulating beauty to mask my emptiness,
But I starved each day like wilting flowers.

I couldn't look at my reflection in the light,
So I only watched myself in the dark;
They passed along their sadness to me,
But they shut their ears off when I spoke,
They told me that they loved me,
But they changed their minds when the alcohol wore off.

So I moulded myself into an artefact,
Polished for meaningless validation,
Dancing in my highest heels,
Wearing the brightest red on my lips.

My body, the only thing that is mine,
It no longer belongs to me;
The sparks that once shone,
Are now gleam of tears,
The curves I adored,
Have become the reason why I despise myself now.

I look in the mirror and
Now I'm just a mosaic of voices and vices,
No amount of wine can fix me,
I'm high on insecurities,
Don't touch me, I may shatter,
Don't speak to me; I may spill venom,

Don't look into my eyes, I might fall,
Just let me be.

One step forward, three steps back

The anxiety becomes tormenting some days;
It creeps all over me and twists into a shadow,
Coming after me until dark,
Until I become a nightmare,
It feels like:

The love I keep waiting for, knowing it's dead,
Roses dried up on my nightstand,
Pills I wish to swallow
To calm the storm in my head,
Often, the road not taken that poets talk about.

I can be laughing with a drink in my hand.
But as soon as it overdoses,
It brings a momentary state of euphoria.

As soon as it wears off,
I go back to mindlessly staring at the ceiling,
Wondering if I'll ever be enough,
Wondering if I will ever be,
The muse of someone's poetry.

Wondering if I'll ever sleep before midnight,
Without rethinking every step I take,
Because it's always one step forward and
Three steps back with anxiety.

It's waking up before sunrise and
Lying in bed until the sun sets.

It's searching for someone
You don't know in a crowd.

It's writing a letter and
Posting it without an address.

It's everything you need but don't want,
And everything in you that's yearning to be alive.

Six degrees of separation

Six degrees of separation tell me,
Everything in this world is connected,
But tell me:
Why are we so distant from ourselves?
Why do we talk about feelings?
When are we better at concealing?

Why do we fall apart?
When is pretending our best forte?
This bizarre anomaly wired in our brains
Tells us to work our fingers to the bone,
To leave love and other emotions to die.

This cathartic feeling in our heart,
Urges us to unfold what we feel,
Thus, we fire daggers in the name of being honest.

This burning sensation inside us,
Asks us to bury our pleasures,
Thus, we unleash a beast within us and destroy each other.

Humanity has lost its faith,
While morals are bent like a sphere,
Love is conditional, and torture is our escape.

Six degrees of separation among us,
Yet, sixty thousand separations within ourselves.

The Arsonist

You cannot convince an arsonist
That he didn't set your home on fire.

Just as you cannot ask someone to love you
When all their love does is damage you.

You cannot anticipate someone to fold an ace of spades
When all you hold are blank-faced cards.

Just as you cannot fight for something
That wasn't yours to begin with.

I miss you. I'm sorry

They say it takes 21 days to form a habit,
But it's five months later,
With seasons changed and lovers gone.

It's time I uncover answers to why,
After all this time,
I can't form the habit of not thinking about him.
When someone talks about love,

I still sense his touch in my palms when I'm cold,
I still recall the first time he held me,
His hands in places where daylight couldn't be.

I still search for his eyes
In every love I come across.
I still feel the solace and safety
When he touches me.
I still go back to December when
Things were fine;
We felt infinity and sounded like ecstasy.

Because you're still the one I want and
You're still the song I can't stop listening to;
I still go back to the night we met,
When we were so in love and so happy;
You're still the one I think of
When they ask me about the love of my life.

These days,
I try to revolt and not think of you that way anymore,
Because you took all of me
And left all of you.

I'm going so wild that I would still run to you,
I would still hold you and remind you of me, of us;

I can't stop thinking about you,
I'm sorry. I know I ended it,
But I still care about you.

We could've had it all

It's a curse, feeling everything at once,
Yet, feeling nothing at all,
How I couldn't feel slight remorse
While losing the love of my life,
But still, I mourn over the boy who was never mine.

How I lie awake,
Wondering what could have been,
Yet my heart didn't flinch once,
As I set myself free from where I shouldn't be.

It's a paradox, seemingly absurd,
To assume I'm fine when I'm clearly not,
To feel all this, praying I didn't,
To not feel what I should feel.

Baby, I'm not in love with you anymore

I make confessions in my head which begin like this:
Baby, I'm not in love with you anymore.

Just waiting for the sake,
I don't want to leave just yet,
I want to know what it feels like
When someone falls out of love,
Consumed by the guilt;
Time never heals,
Feelings die sooner than a candle burns out.

I look at another man,
And wonder how it'd be
To be under him but catch sight of your face;
I people-watch, and my heart gets sick,
To the idea of fixing someone,
Only for them to break you.

I don't want to be the one holding on,
But when we're between the sheets,
I pray time passes like a bullet piercing through a killer's heart.
I once was a soul who believed in love,
But Lord knows I'm made for sin.
I once believed in surrendering for love,
Even God knows I can't sell my soul for validation;
These gut-wrenching car crash feelings,
Along with a lust for a good time,
Makes me realise why love is not enough,
To make someone stay,
And I couldn't stay.

It's midnight again, and I'm not okay again

My heart races from the tears of last night,
My hands tremble from feeling this over again,
I know I am not worth rescuing,
Because all I do is break bridges of love and
Play pretend to be the saint.

They are oblivious, clueless, and unaware,
All I've ever heard are heartthrob speeches,
Echoes of "you're not enough."
All I've ever felt is resentment and rejection.

All I've ever hoped for is someone to tell me
That I am worth climbing mountains for,
Because I hung from cliffs for the ones I loved,
I don't want to remember how it was before;
All I am sure of is that
If someone held me and told me,
"It's going to be okay,"
My heart might not be fine,
But it might feel okay.

Texts that broke me:

1. *"It kills me that I have to say goodbye to you and it feels miserable that I can't scream forever in your ears."*
2. *Texts I never received from you after this.*

Grief and Girlhood

My mother told me it's just a phase,
But I'm still writing verses,
With my misery as the muse.

My therapist told me I needed to ground myself,
So, please instruct me on how to breathe,
Because I'm only familiar with drowning.

My friends told me I was making it about myself;
Tell me, who else am I supposed to make it about?
When it's me who's drowning alone
While all of you just watch my phone ring.

Now every time I close my eyes,
I can't sense what's true anymore;
I'm overdosed on things
I swore I would never get addicted to,
And all I am left with
Are words I can't comprehend.

It's crazy how a nineteen-year-old
Could write so much about grief
Without losing someone alive;
All she ever lost was her girlhood.

Day one without you

Instead of finding
The cold side of the pillow,
I imagined it to be you and
Buried my face in it.

Things I'm afraid of

Fear of not
Being in love but
Being loved;
Healing without falling apart
Cause I fear perfectionism;
"Rolling in the Deep" by Adele
Not being able to look in the mirror
During daylight,
But watching tears
Rolling down my face in the night;
My mind and I,
Memories of him,
Possibility of him returning;
Wondering if I am enough,
Sense of freedom and grief,
Both, from letting it go;
Becoming someone I despise my foes for,
My anger disguised as altruism;
The words I write,
The mess I am,
The muse I create of it.

Let's talk of impossible things

Let's talk of impossible things:
It's impossible for the Earth to go around the sun,
It's impossible for the stars to shine during the day,
It's impossible for me to truly hate you,
It's impossible for you to truly love me,

Never yours to lose, never mine to keep

Dear reader,
You must have heard
"I'm not the woman they love.
I'm the woman before."
Here's my version:

I'm the one who tells them,
"Love conquers all"
While losing my battles alone,
And happily ever after left stranded.

I'm the one who shows them
Love exists with no rules.
While breaking all my rules for them,
I'm the one who gives and provides;
My body is like a mural,
My time as infinite
My heart until it bleeds.

I teach them what love is
Only to end up with no trace of it in me
But traces of their version of love in me;
I end up thinking they are the better man,
Only to realise I fixed them unknowingly.
I lie awake in a bed of love,
Only to feel the starvation of it;
I loathe myself until they validate me
Only to realise I am not the one for them.

You see,
I am never the woman a foolish man can love,
I am a martyr in a foreign land,
Slaughtered and dethroned,

Battling for an empire built of
Everything that isn't mine
To begin and end with.

Questions I often ask myself

Should I long for you without saying a word, or
Has my throat hurt from screaming?
Than having lumps in my throat.
For keeping my silence when I'm thinking of you
Cause I can't stop thinking about you.

Should I summon the courage to erase you
From my memory and unwritten words, or
Get back to living as it was before you
And write to you in the letters I'll never address?

'Cause I would rather have you
Haunt me in places we used to go to
Than not having you in my thoughts anymore.

Should I keep trying to find you in another love, or
Tell you everything I have been hiding
Since your touch electrified me?
'Cause your arms would still feel like
A secure place to be when my world is crumbling down.

Should I hold on to hopes and prayers
That we exist in a multiverse where
We are happy and so in love?
Hold myself together, whispering,
"It's time I set myself free."

So goddamn help me,
I don't want to long for you anymore,
I wanna go home.

I wish this was a love letter

It was never love,
It's been more than 365 days,
Since I chose not to believe it,
Thank you for stepping out,
Never giving me the closure I needed.

Cause I never would have summoned the courage
To admit or understand
That it wasn't really love;
You were just scared to be alone.

If you had asked me six months ago,
I would probably have answered,
That you were the one all along,
But you never asked me the right questions,
And mostly answered my I love yous in lies.

It's six months later now,
I would probably answer.
That is the only thing not right,
Were you for me.

So consider this a love letter,
Loaded with agony, disguised by rage,
For I don't want to knock on doors
Of a house to which I am not invited.

Regrets and Marlboro

I met a boy who's nothing like you,
He doesn't make me laugh like you do,
But his traces surely make me question you.

No, he doesn't give me the gaze
That people who fall in love do,
But he undoubtedly looks at me
Like people watch fireworks on New Year's Day.

Just friends, right?
We whisper to each other;
But in a crowded room,
When I am trying not to fall apart,
I'm thinking of everything but you;
And if we are being honest,
I think of nothing but him.

I have the night tattooed on my mind:
When you broke us like sandcastles on a shore
I ran as far away as I could, questioning myself,
"He's gone forever, is he gone for good?"
But I felt a thrill of escape
When I walked out, as you set me free.

It was a rush so thrilling, such a dream,
Marlboros and tongue-tied with him,
But I forgot dreams are bound to break;
As much as I am guilty as sin,
I don't regret a moment with him.

I was all too well, and you were acquainted

I'm so acquainted with you
I know exactly how you have your tea,
When the clock strikes five,
Five, the number of months I spent
Assuming you were mine.

The songs you hear when quietness is too loud
Are written all over my mind, like a mirror;
Your eyes, a pool of lies
Which I still search for in every lover;
How I was all over you in a crowded room,
Now you're all over me in my memories.

I know you're thinking of me too,
Because you're not half the man
I believed you were;
I know you're waiting for me to crawl to you,
Because you're still a man-child
Who could never love someone.

And don't get me started on
Argumentative confessions of love,
While I had my head in my hands,
Begging for moments of truth.

I know too many people with your name,
Favourite songs I can't listen to anymore,
I can't walk past the places we used to go to
Without picturing you in my arms each morning.

And how my lips are rusted from,
Drags of Marlboro you used to light for me.

But I can't get over the fact of how you pushed away
The love you begged for,
And how you nonchalantly told me
I love you so
As we intertwined in the back of your car,
Where I saw all of me in all of you.

It could never be a blur to me,
Because your memories are tattooed all over me,
Like I'm written all over the lyrics you love,
It was rare; I was there,
I remember it all too well.

I fall asleep on heavy

When no one's watching
I often fall asleep on my left,
For my heart feels too heavy at times,
And I can't breathe some nights;
So I keep switching sides on my bed,
Until I fall asleep, peculiarly dreaming,
Unforeseeably,
I'm detangling my crooked thoughts.
Unwillingly,
I'm searching for air that can't be caught,
Unknowingly,
I'm unalive in wars I never fought.

Secret: I can't sleep most nights

It's when the sun hasn't reached its horizon yet,
When I feel the most alive,
There's chaos and there's tranquillity.

Chaotic,
My mind is replaying my suspicions like a film screen,
My mascara is running down my face as I spread it over
The eyes that saw love bent into indifference.

Tranquillity,
A sense of relief when I wake up,
Without the one who made me a love-fool,
A feeling of nothingness,
Because I've been numb too long to feel anything;
I conceal the nights
I lay awake in pain and pleasure.

What a pleasure to wake up before the world wakes,
But oh, what a pain
To stay awake until the world falls asleep.

Insomnia?
I wouldn't dare to call it,
It's a pain that has been with me,
For as long as I can remember.

I hope you never see me again

The more I have you,
The more I cannot remember about you;
The more I touch you,
The more I mourn you;
The more you look at me,
The more I resent you;
The more you talk to me,
The more I bleed.

As much as I miss having you around,
I hope I never have to be around you again.

Breaking, breathing, isn't it the same?

In nothingness, I pace,
Tired, sad, lonely
I truly feel
Thirty? Forty? Fifty?
I lost count of days.

I guess I've always felt this way
Since I was thirteen
"How many days are seven years?"
Never mind.

Counting days won't make the fact go away,
That I am back in eighth grade,
Tired, sad, lonely
Only this time, I am twenty.

My journals are now published books,
My A grades are rusting somewhere I can't remember,
My best friends are now cigarettes, killing me,
But I feel pretty and sweet,
Now that I have my eyebrows cleaned.

Life was simple when I didn't care about how I looked,
Can't you guess?
It's a cloak to conceal how unpleasant I feel,
Disgust, guilt, regret,
I truly feel.

I am thirteen again
My friends found friends who don't care,
My lovers found love I wished they would,
I am still a ghost, frozen in time,
When my heart was beating, not breaking.

Anxiety: Diagnostic Criteria

As someone who introspects on the human mind,
My head twists into a web of hoaxes,

I'm not convinced if I'm writing symptoms of anxiety or
Penning verses in my memoir.

1.1 Elevated Heart Rate
When I feel the distress stabbing into my soul.

1.2 Sweating
When I'm exhausted from running from my fears.

1.3 Trembling
When I'm writing about what I feel.

1.4 Dissociation
When my lovers reach for my hand.

1.5 Lack of sleep/appetite
When I succumb to insomnia and anorexia.

1.6 Ruminating Thoughts
When I replay the night we met.

1.7 Nausea
When they ask me about the initials I endorsed in the book I wrote.

1.8 Unsteadiness
When I roll over in my sleep and nobody's there.

1.9 Chills & Choking
When I consume the guilt, and my heart is not elevating anymore.

Ask me three wishes

If I were asked three wishes,
I would surrender them,
Just for one prayer to come true; that is,
For someone to hold me when I'm tearing apart.

For it is something no one should go through alone,
And I understand that because
I've seen it in too many eyes;
The loneliness,
The ache and
Restless nights.

And I've been there,
The loneliness,
The ache
Restless nights.

I don't miss you anymore

Even though your initials are embedded
In the book, I wrote about our love,
I must confess there's no remorse for you.

Neither a part of me that needs you
Nor wishful thinking that desires you.

Even though my mum still asks about you,
I must admit I don't miss you at all.

Neither the countless encounters I had with you
Nor the make-up lovemaking I never asked for.

Even though I still preserve the flowers you gave me
I must accept, I always knew you weren't the one.

Neither were you the one to whom I had my allegiance,
Nor were you the reason we were unhappy.

Even though it was I who called it quits,
I must admit you never once made an effort to mend it.

Well, neither did my wistful ego,
Nor your wishful thinking.

Holding knees on the floor

Searching for a minute of silence,
I spent years sprinting from the screams,
Holding my knees on the bathroom floor,
I collect my broken bones from the wars I lost.

I am defeated and worn out,
With my innocence passed on,
Escaping from screams,
Hiding my screams.

It's something about loud voices I cannot fathom;
Ironic, it's what I do when I am choked with anger,
I feed on my defences
Until I'm the loudest woman in the room,
For it's my words I'll take to my grave.

Shutting my ears from being accused of "crazy"
I shut myself off from the lores of ordinary,
Holding my knees on the bathroom floor,
I resuscitate lost ashes into the phoenix of my fears.

I am hunted and being picked on
Piece by piece
Taking me away from peace,
I am lost and set on fire,
It's their favourite scene they so dearly admire.

It's something about the pain,
The addiction
The darkness
The betrayals
I bury everything I love
Until I'm screaming at the graveyard,
Wishing for nothing but for love to be alive again.

Love waits; lust rushes

They say, "Love waits, lust rushes."
Even if you point a gun at me, I wouldn't believe it.

Forgive me, how long can you suffer silently?
Before deciding you don't want to be with the one,
Who loves you to death?

Answer me, make me go crazy, baffle me,
For how many days or months do you long for love
To thrill you, amuse you, and take your breath away,
Before you decide to settle for the bare minimum?

Love waits
Then tell me, how long do I wait,
Before losing my sanity?
Answer my questions, please,
Make me understand how to long for someone
When it's the only thing you cannot do,
Physically, spiritually, and emotionally, too.

Lust rushes
Then tell me, how quickly can I unrecall
The moments I didn't want to be under him, but I was?
Answer me, satisfy me.
How to not find transcendence
When someone you don't love anymore is tracing you
Like the hands of an artist, with you being the muse?

Love waits; lust rushes,
Don't we all rush into writing a love tale,
While waiting so lovingly for the trace of lust?

Crawling on my limbs

Let's get your therapist,
She would need a therapist for this,
You only wish to heal, internally screeching,
But he was never a fan of girls who talked about feelings.

Let's be honest:
You don't need him.
You just admire the way his hands fit around your waist,
How he lies and always makes you wait.

Let's face it:
You're not delusional and wild,
He's just not the love of your life,
He'll end up saying the same things to his future wife.

Let's talk about it:
You're not his girlfriend
And he was never your friend;
He's just not a man who can accept,
You can't write a story with an empty ink,
Just as he couldn't love you without his drink.

Let's be real:
Trust me, you can survive without him,
He just wants you to crawl to him,
One insulted four limbs.

On accepting myself

It took me 150 weeks to recognise myself,
To glance in the mirror and declare,
"Shut out those voices and love yourself."
So I lingered in silence and grieved,
And this is a story of how I healed.

Their words turned me numb like anaesthetics,
So I disguised myself in cosmetics,
Only talk with numbers in mathematics,
And circled my pain into something poetic.

My eyes lingered on models in magazines,
Cried myself to sleep for weeks in quarantine;
They saw my body but left my misery unseen,
How could I grow up and recover? I was just fifteen.

At sixteen, I was struggling with low self-esteem,
Shattered dreams and silenced screams,
Wore large-sized attire so I couldn't be seen,
My tears inscribed stories unforeseen.

From the overachiever to maturing into a mess,
The boys I loved and friends I had couldn't care less,
Grew out of my favourite jeans and dress,
So I quit eating because of the distress.

At seventeen, comparison devoured me,
I attempted to become someone I knew I could never be,
"I am not enough."
Even my anxiety could agree.

Weeks turned into years, and all I had left were my tears,
But my words of pain reached a thousand ears;
So I switched from the elevator to the stairs,
I quit all the beers and freed myself from fears,

And I finally could look myself in the mirror.

At twenty, I'm happier than ever,
I'm still trying. Is it easy? No, never.

On the edge

I'm my father's daughter,
I have a compulsion to get rid of things,
In a selfish, effortless, nonchalant way;
Easy to let go when you're the one leaving,
Leaving the love of your life,
Life, you imagined you would have had.

Had I known I couldn't fix him,
I would never have dared to break him.

I'm also my mother's daughter,
Fixating on mending what is thrown out,
It's never an easy thing,
To give life to what you didn't end,
End or begin, does it matter anyway?

Anyhow, the poem's getting intimate
Did I mention I love to stand on the edge of exit gates?

THE MUSE

Writer's Block

What am I going to write about today?
Human touch,
Conversations with the mirror,
Backspace,
Overcorrections,
Cigarettes I swore I wouldn't touch,
Long paragraphs or a quintet?
Free verse or a rhyming scheme?
Google, what rhymes with sadness?
Mama, why do I exist?
Is my heart apathetic, or
I cannot turn feelings into words anymore,
What if my ex-lover's mother still asks about me?
Why is that anorexia beginning to feel good?
Parentheses begin,
This is me trying,
Parentheses end.
Maybe a letter to my lover.
Saying "fuck you" for treating me this way.
A note for when my therapist can't heal my depression.
Paragraph change.
Select all.
Delete.

Hurt people hurt people

I overheard someone the other day
Saying, "Pain changes people."
I wondered if that was true,
Yes, it does.
I've been compelled by pain
More than I've been nurtured by love,
I've spent my nights in the dark,
Than my days in the rays.

Bitterness has been my companion,
Overshadowing most glimpses of love,
Denial has been my protection,
Making my reality unbearable.

When all is said and done,
Once you know what pain is,
It's hard to surround yourself with love.

Once you choose to dwell in the dark,
It's hard to uncover daylight
Once you admit that you're not in pain,
Healing becomes impossible.

Pain changes you.
It makes you long for something,
You know you will never return;
It traps you,
Causing you to linger in memories of the past,
Making your present a blur,
It turns your existence into estrangement,
Twisting your dreams into nightmares.

I don't know what destiny holds for me,
All I know right now is that,
I'll never be the same.

Love, it's so consuming

I've always wondered,
How people realise they have found love,
For me, this realisation has been quite different.

I knew I was in love when
I stood in a diner queue
And he held my hand because,
I panicked in social situations.

He was ripping tiny pieces from the receipt,
While I crumbled and rolled the leftovers,
I knew it wasn't love, but
Anxiety keeps us together.

And that was the moment the voices in my head
Wondered about the side of love
That no one dares to talk about.

It's the type of love that keeps you awake at night,
Because you are questioning your place in their life;
The type of love that makes you forget everything,
Because it's all that devours you.

It's the type of love that asks you nothing,
Because all it does is massacre you recklessly;
It's the type of love where you listen to their music,
For validations you never receive.

The type of love that weighs heavily on your heart,
But brings you short-lived solace;
The type of love that intoxicates you with daggers,
Stealing every glimpse of happiness;
It's the love that leaves you bare,
With nothing to spare and nothing to feel.

Denial is better than desire

It's been six months and countless days
Since I've talked or written about how I feel;
Silence is comforting these days,
Denial is better than desire,
Words I used to write only exist in my mind,
Loss is my best friend these days;
I'm mourning someone I don't know anymore,
I'm longing for someone whom I know won't return,
It's me, six months and countless days ago.

Oh, to be in love

To have someone hold you amidst storms,
To have a hand that fits flawlessly in yours,
To know you have a reason to arrive home,
To have an escape from your worst fears.

Oh, to lose that once-in-a-lifetime love,
To be standing alone in hurricanes,
To be so deprived of touch,
To be so deprived of something called comfort
That you don't want anyone to take care of you anymore,
Because you're too scared,
From bleeding in love so many times,
That you run from what you know is right and easy.

It's over; you're still here

It's absurd how I am over you,
No, I haven't forgotten how,
You can't fall asleep in absolute darkness,
And I have certainly not forgotten
How you love the words
I put down in letters I used to write to you.

I can see you keeping an eye on my Instagram
Because I specifically posted for you;
No, I haven't forgotten your phone passcode,
And definitely not the fact,
That your face could still unlock my phone.

Because if I make the effort to remove you
From everywhere you used to be,
I would have to erase my entire life,
So it's crazy how I am over you
But you're still here,
In every face, I come across,
And everywhere I go.

Flowers, they wilt and wither

"What's your favourite flower?"

"I don't know. I loved the subtle beauty of red roses."
Until I saw my first love giving them to his new love.

I used to adore white roses when I saw my sister's boyfriend,
Give them to her every time they went out.

I admired daffodils and baby's breath,
When I wore them at her wedding.

I always desired that someday, someone would care to bring me flowers

When the love of my life brought me red roses on Valentine's Day,
I rediscovered my love for the colour red,
But our love, like the roses, didn't last long.

And to be brutally honest,
I want to scream fuck you to the boy who never got me flowers,
But it got me addicted to the thorns.

But to answer your question,
I still have every flower that every boy has ever given me,
In a box titled flowers may wilt and wither, I pray love never does.

I can't tell you what my favourite flower is,
For I am afraid I don't want you to wilt and wither in my box too.

In my head

In my head, your shirt is absorbing my tears
As I am lying on your heart in my room
Where it's just us at midnight,
Stargazing from where we're laying.

In my head, I get closure,
A goodbye lovemaking,
We listen to the night we met.
When you're telling me the truth,
Instead of enchanting me with,
Bittersweet
Sugarcoated
Manipulative lies.

In my head, we're dancing in the kitchen,
Nothing but your shirt on;
We burned the cake in the oven
Cause we were too busy remembering,
Remembering, my scent all over you,
Whispers of 'forever' in my ears.

In my head, you tell me you love me,
Because you mean it
Not to fuck me in your bed of lies
Until you're satisfied.

In my head, you're not the
Machiavellian
Self-absorbed
Narcissist,
But you're someone I can truly cry with,
Not just in my head.

The Parking Lot

There are poems scattered throughout my life,
Which I can never write,
Love stories unwritten,
Moments uncaptured,
They begin and end in the parking lot.

Twitching and butterflies,
Right before my very first kiss,
And running back home,
Praying, replaying these words:
"I hope this never ends."

Moments of intimacy
That felt like sacred heaven,
Whispers of "I love you."
During the song, it talks about
Dying for the one you love.

Screaming, moaning,
"I don't want to leave just yet."
And him asking me to stay,
Knowing he wasn't the one,
Yet, choosing to stay.

Beginning of beautiful stories,
Ended with tales of a broken heart,
A heart, that wasn't mine,
To fool a heart that wasn't mine either,
Led to losing everything in a blink,
All in the parking lot.

Regrets, grief, pain; it's art

Do you recall
How you gasped for air
And couldn't breathe?
Choked with intoxication
Of your own choices,
Of your own thoughts;
You couldn't recall
Who you were and where you were.

You reached for salvation,
Dangling through a rustic thread
Made of regret
Built by grief
And you fell so hard
No one heard you weep.

Do you recall
Waking up in the middle of the night
And not being able to reflect
If it were all real or just a fantasy?
But when you woke up
With no one in your bed
And nothing inside your head.
Did you wonder if it doesn't matter?
Because it was all that once mattered.

You were just a kid
Journaling your way through pain,
Who built a home out of a house
In pages that people now read
Because your home was just walls to you
And the ink was your saviour,
Which is why
They love the stories you tell aloud now.

You're now twenty-something,
And you only find comfort in
A glass of wine and
Men who could distract you
From the misery you are;
It may seem poetic
But you know it's killing you.

You're so addicted to betrayal
You don't know what faith is;
You're so conditioned to believe
You're not worthy of love;
Something you could hold onto
That you stay awake until 4 AM
Falling in love with
Shadows of your worst fears.

But darling,
You have to break free and learn not to break apart;
Please remember the places and people you love,
There are dreams you have yet to fall in love with,
Hands yet to hold and hearts yet to heal.

Please, hold on,
You have unwritten words inside you,
With sounds of laughter yet unheard,
Your patience can't give in just yet,
You have to walk another thousand miles now.

Muse as fine as him

When I begin to describe him,
My words descend,
My lips part,
My voice shatters,
And my heart sprints;
He's much more than
I can ever call a lover.

His skin is daylight,
His eyes are so enchanting,
His lips taste like
My favourite cigarette
And his hands imprinted
My body like it isn't mine.

When his beautiful brown eyes
Encounter mine when we're intertwined;
When he lingers a little longer
As we kiss in his car;
I stutter and struggle
In the process of describing him
Because I have never had a muse
As fine as him.

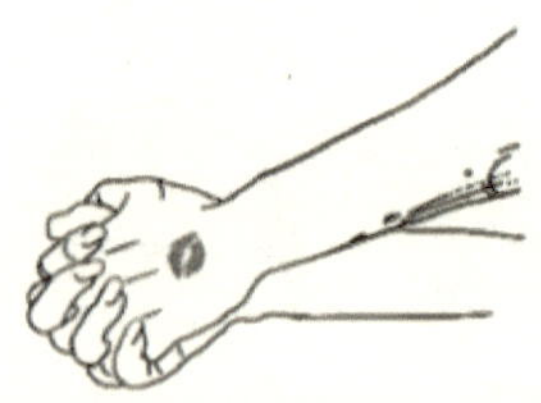

My freedom has never been free

As a woman,
My freedom has never been free.

In the night when the stars light up,
I am asked to lose my shimmer,
And sleep under a roof
That reeks of emptiness.

When the sun ascends,
I am asked to polish myself,
To put on a pretend face so fetching
That my screams become voiceless.

When people come over,
At the parties
Even if I am bleeding,
Or mourning the loss of a loved one,
I am asked to lose my comfort
So the men could pour whiskey
And mock the work we do for them.

As a lover,
I am anticipating to lose my identity
In the name of compromise.
As a daughter,
I am expected to recollect the mess
When voices are raised in my parents' bedroom.

As a wife,
I am ready to bring dinner to the table
When the man brings money
And unsatisfactory pleasure.

As a mother,
I am expected to lose my youth

Just so my daughter can scream fuck you at me
When she is my age.

It's a story of her,
About the sacrifice of her,
Told by you, written by me.

My freedom has never been free;
It has always been a price paid for.

I'm a mosaic of memories

I am made of
Words never spoken and
Memories that starved in my head,
Faces I could never unlearn,
And the flicker of hands;
I could recognise it anywhere.

When I step back,
Watch my life through screens,
I realise I am a mosaic of everything,
I have worshipped and relinquished,
I've had blood all over my hands,
Bleeding myself dry
From not being able to breathe
And drowning in nothingness.
You see, I am made of infinity.

Unsaid speeches, I want to scream,
Handful of unconfessed love
That turned to resentment;
Incomplete poems in my drafts
Keeping me awake at midnight
Space between the ones I love
And bridges of love I broke,
Just to crawl back when I found myself alone.

And again,
Everything I have ever loved,
Everything I have ever lost.

I miss how you knew me

It's me, hi. The love of your life,
Or you can call me the one who got away,
I miss you;
Not in the
"I want to be with you" way
But, I miss how you knew me.

I miss you,
Not in the
"I want to hold you as you break down" way,
But I miss how I used to be your safe place.

I miss you,
Not in the
"I want you to text me" way,
But I miss how you never not answered me.

I miss you,
Not in the
"I can't hear our songs anymore" way,
But I miss how you knew all the lyrics.
To all my favourite songs.

I must confess, these last couple of months
Haven't been as easy
As I have pretended.

I have unforeseen the grief of your footsteps,
Leaving my front porch,
Having my heart stabbed with goodbye.

As much as I want your fingers
Intertwined between my freezing palms,
As much as my ears have gone cold-blooded,
Wanting to hear you call out my name,

I know running back to the past,
Just because it feels familiar,
Would be a disastrous (beautiful) mistake.

Skins and spirits

She never belonged to anyone,
Her heart mended by a couple of hands,
Broken by the same,
Always made her believe it was love.

She's the girl who fell in love with
Men who never wanted her,
Who turned her into a woman
Boys always want.

She never repulsed
Love, mostly unrequited,
Skin, caressed inside out,
Spirit, mostly deserted,
Tears, never effaced.

She could never belong to anyone,
Who only belongs to herself.

Falling in love with you

Flushed cheeks, adrenaline,
Anxiety disguises butterflies,
Electrifying pounding while making love,
Stolen glances and captivating stares.

"I wish I had kissed him."
"Are you real? Is this happening?"
"Please linger a little longer when our lips meet."
"Did you reach home safely?"

For all my crumbled castles,
And all your sceptic fears,
For all my lipstick smudges on your cigarettes.
And your kisses on my neck.

May you know the rest.

Love I want is not the love I need

I'm not the one you can wake beside
I like my bed empty and waking alone,
I'm not the one who holds you in a hospital grey,
I pray for you in the most hideous way.

I'm not the one whom you take home to mother;
I devour all kinds of love,
Never wishing for forever.

For long, I thought
I deserved a love that was thrilling,
Passionate enough,
To consume me to the point,
Where I couldn't breathe.

Love, that would put me on top,
But wouldn't catch me when I fall;
Love that made me question my stars,
That made me gaze at the moon for hours,
In search of daylight,
Only for me to burn and ignite.

It took me a hundred sleepless nights,
Hundred and one tears to realise:
The love I want may not be the love I need.

I need a love that waits for me,
Patient enough
To heal me in ways I don't ask for;
Love, that would hold me
When the world is against me, giving me life.

Love, that makes me fall in love with
Waking up by a lover's side;
Taking my breath away,

While giving me oxygen,
It's painful to breathe.

Love, that wouldn't let me bleed,
Free of affairs and greed;
I wouldn't have to search for daylight,
For I need a love
Where I don't have to wonder whys and mights
And a lover who could take me home to his mother.

Homesick

I'm homesick for a home I don't have.
Friends, I walk past the hallway,
Love of my life that found love last May,
Mint tea I used to have with him every Friday,
A family that now lives worlds away.

I have worlds inside me I could never sway,
From nights, I couldn't make them stay.

Does it matter?
In the blink of an eye, it all went away.

For love, I'd die

But for love, I'd die,
Ignite myself even if it's lies,
Tracing the skies
Searching for our signs;
For love, I'd watch myself bleed dry,
Intoxicating myself with highs,
Because love never answers my whys;
If they ask me, against gravity I'd fly,
For love, books I'd write,
Even when I know it isn't right,
But for love, I'd always fight.

For love, I'd live

But if I were grabbing my last breath
I would only recall love;
Not the times
I had my heart in someone's hands
Smashing castles on my homeland's sands
I wouldn't remember.
How I was on pins and needles my whole life
Or how all my words feel like a twisted knife.
Lately, all my breaths are at rock bottom,
Gasping for love I cannot fathom,
Because if I were taking my last breath right now,
I would hold on to love so hard,
That to be unalive would seem so lively.

Evergreen, our group of friends

That's what love feels like
When fifteen people laugh across a room,
Hiding liquor, maybe one or two secret affairs,
We were happy; we were fine,
We aged well like wine.

Love, unconditional turned unrequited,
Will be eternally written
In books, I am yet to write.

Dreams, applauded and unfulfilled,
Still wished for
Despite us being strangers.

Tears wiped, but sometimes concealed,
Paved the way for hugs that felt like home.

Hope, taken and given,
Still gives me strength;
When I think of good times,
In my hard times

It's a lump in my throat,
To think we could have had it all.
Love, life, and laughs we imagined.

My home is now a house
That doesn't send invites anymore;
I don't clean up the bottles when everyone leaves,
Instead, I replay the cheers in my head.
As my heart grieves.

I often sleep facing the pictures
Framed on my nightstand
Which remind me of dancing in ecstasy

That my heart couldn't withstand;
While spilling the gin we so dearly loved,
With friends who felt like my own blood.

Echoes of laughter exist inside my head,
Along with backspaced text,
I write unaided in my bed,
Oaths and secrets kept like religion,
Yet some apologies left unforgiven.

My words suffice the void of closure never conferred
My eyes withhold visions of the past blurred,
Whilst I reassure myself by reciting:
We are all in different, maybe better places.

In the same town but running through paces,
Maybe that's what they warned us about,
When they asked us to never grow up,
Cause now I cheer with an empty cup.

"Evergreen are our group of friends, don't think we'll say that word again."

December I remember

There's something crestfallen about December,
Something surreal, so feral
Maybe it's the way I left my tears
On my lover's shirt
Or Lover by Taylor Swift,
I can't listen without hurt;
Maybe it's the mint I always want in my tea,
Or thirst for the one who had it with me.

Most of all, it's the way a part of me feels unalive,
It's a lifeless, nonchalant feeling I can't describe,
Like searching for movie tickets in a sold-out show,
Or feeling nothing sitting by the afterglow,
Visions of the past blurred in sight,
Asking myself,
Was it ever real? Will it ever be real?

It's the new year's countdown that sinks me truly,
Why do we celebrate the beginning
But never what's ending?
For it's only the ending that creates
The most beautiful poetry.

Why do we anticipate love just made for two,
But never love that's unconditional?
For it's
Oh, how the wine always takes away the blues.

She is in love again, folks

I can't count on my fingers
The number of times
I've been deluded by love.
Delusion,
I wouldn't say
Rather, muse imprinted on pages I write.

I was a love-fool
Lovestruck by
Lovesick beloveds
While you were hiding in plain sight all along.

My hands on your neck,
Yours on my thigh
As we drive by the sunset sky;
I light your cigarette,
While you light up my despair
You love me so in all my fairness.

Your smirking face when I call your name,
Makes me forget love for me was once a game,
We're in your car, and my thoughts are
Of when we're in my room,
Recalling when we fell in love in the month of June.
Now you hold me in a crowded room,
As I hold your anxieties,
Leaving me in a state of high in my sobriety,
It's passion and undying chemistry,
When it's him, I feel ecstasy.

In not-so-loving memory of

I would engrave my thoughts into pages like a tattoo,
Never letting them fade,
Like an art gallery exhibiting its best art,
Designed with frantic hands and hysterical minds,
But I am so tired of pacing, chasing, running, writing words,
In memory of the ones,
Who wouldn't say a word to me,
If they ever saw me again?

And then I stopped writing about you

These may be the final words I put down
In the memoir of your memories,
Knowing I'll regret you,
Written all over my stories.

Your face will continue to remain my peace,
Even when I see you only in my dreams,
Like my hand will always be a city away,
When you long for me to hold you.

But I hope I am miles away,
I wish that you aren't wishing,
To accidentally running into me.

I will persist with the thought of being in love with you,
Knowing you're a wine stain I can never obliterate,
But as much as I think of you,

I hope I never have to be the one you think of
When you slip across your most recalled lyric.
"Take me back to the night we met."

Because I've fallen for boys
Who put me on a pedestal,
For writing narratives about them;
But you, oh you
Who called me crazy when you weren't the muse
I hope I never have to write about you ever again.

Instruction Manual: How To Love Me

1. Tell

Tell me you love me so you can't breathe,
Tell me how my absence aches you,
Tell me how I can make your life happier,
Tell me how you can't sleep unless you hear my voice.

2. Remember

Remember the phrases I write,
Remember the films I mentioned,
Remember the songs I play in your car,
Remember my coffee order even though I have coffee once every three months.

3. Do

Do make me laugh when I call you crying,
Do grab my hand when we're in public,
Do kiss me when I hug you a little longer,
Do the things, even if inconsequential, just to see me laugh.

And if it all comes off too much,
Just take the long route
When you're dropping me home;
I'll know.

Caution: Fragile; handle with care.

You're worth the risk

I'm a writer,
I write about everything in my head and heart,
But it's an anomaly that,
The only thing I can't write about is you.

For it's the stability I feel,
I don't feel the need to pen my despair,
Or scribble my emptiness into pages.

For it's the way I feel heard,
I don't have the impulse to cry my heart out
Or hush my midnight thoughts.

For it's the way you see me,
I don't want to paint my life in screaming colours
Or savour the mediocrity of black and white hues.

For it's you who are my balance,
I don't want to romanticise being love-bombed,
Or being put up on a pedestal.

For what it's worth,
It's you.
For what it's worth,
It's us.

For you, I would surrender

For the hypocrites, I wouldn't bend,
But I'm on my knees for you,
I surrender myself yet again,
In the game of love, we so dearly love.

I'm running from sanity yet again,
Your hands crumbling me in thin air;
I've fallen, turned into dust.

Running through visions in my head,
I recall every time we're in my bed;
I close my eyes and don't feel the need
To cater to thoughts that don't let me sleep.

And when you drive through the winter mist,
As you pull me tighter,
That's when I draw my name into your wrist,
Like you entice yours on my lips.

The hypocrites, I wouldn't believe,
But I'll let you carry all my faith on your fingertips,
I surrender myself yet again.

You're not your fears or failures

I can't love someone like me,
I don't know how they do it,
Self-acclaimed prodigy who is weak,
So weak, I don't even feel remorse
Deluded by desires of vanity,
It's mundane for me how I don't feel sanity.

I think they are the greatest,
For when I have tears to share,
The best, when far-ranging fears I cannot bear,
Missed calls with Marlboros;
Thank God, they care for my sorrows.

In moments like these, I admire my lover
And the family, by blood and chosen,
"You're not your fears or failures,
You do so well compared to your peers."
They keep chanting as my heart keeps shattering.

How can I not fear when all my life I've never gone wrong?
What if one day the world's ending?
I'm defeated, fallen, and nowhere to be found.
Would you still expect me to save the world, or
Would you rather want me to save myself?

I know, I know, it's what I love to be,
But do you really love something if it makes you miserable?

So I'll spill a secret,
I don't want to be me anymore;
You could tear my flesh and take my fears,
For, give me for a moment of fresh air,
I don't want to be a mosaic of anticipations,
I just want to be me.

This isn't about me

They say cold winds often precede hail storms,
It's why passion seems electric at first glance
While anticipation makes you burn,
Desire masquerades itself as love.

Soon enough,
Twin flames burn into ashes of separation,
The undying passion turns into cynicism,
While love turns into something you can't reach for.

One fine day, you dream of killing someone,
The next day, your lover leaves you stranded
He declares he will die if you don't love him.
But takes pleasure in boozing with another woman.

Wait, the story isn't about me.

But the storm always arrives at the worst time,
It's when passion turns into desperation,
While your youth begins to feel caged;
You reject invitations and write in your room,
It's why you rarely feel pleased, always doomed.

You hear the news; they are calling you a bitch,
Until you realise being a bitch is a privilege,
And the story is, in fact, about you.

They say a cold wind often precedes hailstorms,
But they never warned about the affliction.

Summer of my life

It's the cold mist that makes it hard to breathe,
Lost nights and fire that can't keep me warm,
I am frozen in time with chokes and chills,
But you are the summer of my life.

It's your warm embrace that makes me feel like
I am a child in the summer sun;
Feral, carefree, so exhilarated,
If you're a summer sun in June,
Who needs New Year's and December anyway?

I'll run away and meet you at a beach,
Build a sandcastle with bare hands,
Just to destroy trying to cover ourselves in it;
If it's you taking my youth
Who needs innocence anyway?

It's the way you hold me that reminds me,
You are the summer of my life;
It's not a season, just indescribable reasons,
If summer means being with you,
I would let myself freeze even if it's hard to breathe.

The Limelight

As a child, I desired nothing more than
Being the spotlight
If not, being in it.

I recall the mornings at school,
When I wanted nothing but the feeling of
Racing to the stage and watching the crowd
Applaud for me and appreciate me.

I recall the yearning for a great crowd glaring at me,
Accompanied by an intense desire for
Watching over each face in the crowd,
Letting them know it's okay to be eaten up by stage fright,
Cause once you're in the spotlight,
The thrill takes over the terror.

I also remember getting the chance to
Stepping onto the stage and
Finally getting the chance.
To read a poem I wrote.

In that instant, I froze;
I couldn't utter a single word and
I wanted nothing but to run away and hide,

I remember the little girl,
Striving to get rid of what she always wanted.

I remember the perplexed child,
Questioning her worth as she left behind her heartfelt dream.

I remember the baffled crowd.
Gossiping: "She must've been crazy to throw it away."

I remember how I felt exactly;

A rush so unnerving, leaving me empty,
A high so conniving, I felt like losing my mind.

Let me end this tale in six words:
That's what loving him felt like.

The End

It's not worth it if it doesn't burn your soul and consume you. It's also not worth it if all it does is consume your soul and burn you out.

www.ingramcontent.com/pod-product-compliance
Lightning Source LLC
LaVergne TN
LVHW091118150826
845673LV00002B/881

* 9 7 9 8 8 9 5 5 6 7 0 0 5 *